THE
GARDENS
AT
TEMPLE SQUARE

THE GARDENS AT TEMPLE SQUARE

The four seasons

by

Lynn McGhie

PHOTOGRAPHS BY LYNN MCGHIE, ZEKE MCGHIE, JIM KENT, AND DRAKE BUSATH
BOOK DESIGN BY LYNN MCGHIE
LYNN MCGHIE ASSOC. PUBLISHERS

*This book is dedicated to all who do and have contrib-
uted to the gardens at Temple Square--a brave and
generous bunch. Their caring and resourceful spirits
give the gardens the joyful expression that brings us all
such pleasure throughout the year.*

Acknowledgements

I wish to express my sincere appreciation to those who have been helpful and supportive in the creation of this book. My wife, who has supplied me with the names of flowers and plants, has been my main critic throughout the project. Her wonderful positive attitude has helped me through the discouraging stages of the journey.

Others have been generous with their time and talent: Borge Andersen with his suggestions concerning the photography; Lance Turner my mentor; Carolee Harmon and Jeri Parker with their editing and rewriting skills; Peter Lassig, at who's feet I learned about flower combinations, sputter, and the true expression of the Creator; and the stewards who, without even knowing it, provided valuable information in our conversations about the gardens. To Elaine, Florence, Ruth, Jackie, and Barbara, who gave encouragement and expressed faith in the project; and to Mr. and Mrs. Norm Tanner, who helped get the project off the ground financially, I owe a debt of gratitude. All are dear and wonderful friends whom I love and respect.

Finally, I wish to thank my children, Melissa and Zeke, who kept my office running competently and to Skip Zenger who gathered together the photographs from my archives. Without them or any of the above, the book could not have become a reality.

CONTENTS

2

The gardens at TEMPLE SQUARE are among the world's finest. As with all gardens, they are constantly changing. They are spectacular during every season, even in winter when the Square is filled with half a million tiny lights.

If you enjoy gardening or love the beauty of flowers, come along and view these magnificent offerings.

TEMPLE SQUARE

3

Lynn McGhie

Preface

William Wagstaff was among the early pioneers to arrive in the Salt Lake Valley. He came in the fall of 1853. A horticulturist by trade, he staked out his farm and nursery in what is now downtown Salt Lake City. William planted many of the trees that first shaded the pioneer settlement.

In his personal journal, William records the trials he experienced at the time of his conversion and later as a pioneer in the "valley of the mountains." His travels from England to the West were made at enormous sacrifice: he lost eighteen members of his immediate family to the ravages of influenza, cholera, and scarlet fever. Yet his faith in Mormonism was unwavering. That faith and his talent as a horticulturist were significant factors in creating a love for beautifying the young town. The grounds at Temple Square are the fullest expression of that love.

William Wagstaff was my great grandfather. I am proud of his courage and grateful for his gift in helping to green our desert valley.

The Gardeners

Many have contributed to the beauty and peace of the gardens at Temple Square. They cover approximately 25 acres in downtown Salt Lake City and include the Church Administration Building, the Church Office Building, The Relief Society Building, the Beehive and Lion Houses, the Joseph Smith Memorial Building and two small cemeteries nearby: the Kimball and Brigham Young.

The gardeners are as dedicated as any workers I have ever known. They are few in number but great in work ethic. These men and women believe that their contributions are of great worth in presenting The Church of Jesus Christ of Latter-day Saints to the world. The results are inspired by the tireless effort of head gardener, Peter Lassig, who has spent the better part of his life designing, creating, and tending these beautiful and endearing gardens. His loving care for both the gardens and their gardeners is felt throughout.

Peter's dazzling combinations using annuals and perennials are unlike any others. He has developed a philosophy about the use of trees, shrubs and flowers that is unique. The gardens reflect his ability to recognize the greatness and majesty of God and nature, and he works enthusiastically to express that in ways others can enjoy.

FALL

Fall is a time of transition. As leaves turn and the gardens are readied for next spring's showing, little is left of all the color that so recently filled them.

Here daisy chrysanthemums are blooming in early November. Already there has been a light dusting of snow, but frost has not yet darkened them. The air is cool and when the sun is shining, the days are perfect for working the soil.

8

all always brings such a wonderful display of color! The canyons surrounding the Salt Lake Valley blaze with bright, yellow aspen and flame-colored scrub oak. These trees and shrubs, against the dark green pines and the wheat-colored grass, create stunning vistas. The Rocky mountains protect these valleys from the extreme cold air masses that plunge down from Canada into the heartland of Colorado, Montana, Kansas, and further east.

Here, Bechtel Crab Apple trees flame into florescent beauty to signal the certainty of fall.

9

Chrysanthemums, cabbages, and blue salvia unite their wonderful colors. The chrysanthemums add no more than green foliage during the summer, but as temperatures cool, these burst forth giving the gardens a final glory. Ornamental cabbages grow larger and more luxuriant during summer until the first frost. The combination of pink, purple, and green is irresistible. The chrysanthemums are expected but the cabbages are a charming surprise.

II

October--and the leaves are falling. A last burst of color is seen in the impatiens blooming along the east wall of the area immediately surrounding the Temple (left). The crab apple trees are loaded with shiny red fruit, and the catalpa trees are showing yellow leaves under the still-green top foliage.

This is the time of year anemone japonica come into their own and brighten dark garden corners.

13

14

It's early morning on Temple Square. From the doorway of the Assembly Hall, the gardens appear to be at rest. Fall is in the air and the misty outline of the temple spires are seen over the now-changing leaves. In the next few days, summer plants will be removed and replaced with pansies, and tulip, daffodil, and hyacinth bulbs. The pansies will add what little color is to be seen during the dismal winter months. As the snow melts, these bright little "Fantasia" faces appear announcing that spring is really going to come.

Snow usually arrives in the valley some time in November. Preparations have already begun for the coming lighting spectacle. This is a feverish time for the gardeners because the transition from summer to spring planting must be completed before the first snow arrives. The gardens have been so full of color that this stage of development seems strange indeed.

15

The Church of Jesus Christ of Latter-day Saints holds a worldwide conference during the first week of October. The summer gardens are at their height of beauty during this first week in October so it seems almost reckless to begin pulling out the summer annuals as soon as conference is over. It would seem reasonable to allow them to languish and be themselves for the rest of the season, but spring gardens must be planted before snow and frost hit, so out they come.

Normally it takes about six weeks for the regular small staff of gardeners to pull summer blooms, prepare the beds, and plant next year's bulbs, pansies, and other spring flowers. But in 1993 a new method was initiated. Volunteers from nearby congregations came to assist with the planting. The first Saturday 500 fathers and sons came to help in the removal of the summer annuals under the direction of the gardening staff.

The next week 500 mothers and daughters arrived to do the planting. The morning was cold and wet, but these volunteers stayed and worked until the job was completed. The gardeners were buoyed up not only by their help but by their demonstration of faith and dedication.

17

18

This is the Lion House, and it is used today as a reception center. The cottage gardens are similar to those that might have been growing when Brigham Young and his family lived here. They shed a poetic brightness on the home.

During the summer, these gardens are often a subject for local artists. As seen here, however, the summer flowers have been pulled out, and the garden is now ready for the team of planters. The designers have thrown the bulbs and pansies on top of the soil. Seen in the foreground are the last of the tall pink hollyhocks. Behind the fence, lavender and roses continue blooming. Climbing the light fixture and fence are morning glory vines.

19

Just inside the east gate of the Square in the foreground of the Temple, are seen the bottom branches of one of the few Cedars of Lebanon in the entire valley.

The Temple wears a mantle of holiness to members of the Church who perform labors of love here for their families. It is a house of worship, a house of prayer.

Chrysanthemums remain to provide a spot of color in this bed south of the Tabernacle.

21

All silver and white, the Temple, the grounds, and the Tabernacle appear in repose. While nature seems to be at rest, the gardeners are far from still as they work rapidly to finish stringing the myriads of lights, that will turn Temple Square into a wonderland of nighttime color.

Preparations for this extravaganza begin in September when lights are tested and replaced in readiness for limbs and branches. The Friday night after Thanksgiving they will explode into starlight, and the grounds will come alive.

No one is ever disappointed. A life-size creche will be displayed, and the message of Christmas will be broadcast on the large lawn north of the Tabernacle. There will be programs, concerts, and messages for all-the faithful, the learned, and the seekers.

23

24

Since fall is usually one of Salt Lake's wetter seasons, those putting up the lights are often working in the rain, sleet or snow. One thing is sure! Putting up the lights cannot be postponed for fair weather. To the left and below are a couple of the brave augmented staff members adding lights to the trees and shrubs. They are dressed in yellow rain slickers to keep dry.

WINTER

Winter on Temple Square is a time of strong contrasts--festive, bleak; stimulating, quiet; comforting, cold. It can sparkle with the laughter of youth or be reflective with the stillness of meditation. During the Christmas season, Temple Square is full of families: old and older, young and younger--the youngest on Daddy's shoulders or in Mother's arms--all coming to be overwhelmed by lights and touched by the messages of Christmas.

Nightly concerts given in the Tabernacle or the Assembly Hall are filled to capacity. It is a place where shoppers wander to feel the Christmas spirit and admire the glittering lights. As snow covers the ground, the earth gathers strength for the gardens to come. It is a time for evaluating last year's successes and disappointments, ordering seeds, growing new summer plants, and making commitments for an even more glorious new year of gardens.

28

tringing Christmas lights requires time and patience. Workers wire limbs and branches so carefully that each individual tree is defined. The effect is stunning! A stroll through the square is its own reward. The scene is another tribute to the stewards who labor diligently through the coldest of days into the nights to create this wonderland of brilliance.

een through the trees in its simple tower, the Nauvoo Bell sounds the hour and is a reminder of more difficult times in the history of the early Saints. In 1847 when the pioneers arrived in the Great Salt Lake Valley, this territory was a retreat, a place of peace and renewal.

vening falls on the square. As the sky darkens, the Christmas lights come on and visitors fill the walkways. Singers from various youth choirs chatter noisily as they gather to participate in holiday programs. Christmas carols from the Tabernacle Choir softly fill the air and there is a feeling of peace as high-stuccoed walls shut out the sounds of a bustling city.

The Temple against a black velvet sky is dramatic indeed. The accompanying lights are a beautiful contrast to the solid granite walls they frame. On top of the center-front spire to the east is a statue of Moroni, an ancient prophet of the Book of Mormon. He is blowing a horn to usher in the last great period of time before the second coming of Jesus Christ and the final thousand years of the earth's existence.

33

S P R I

Spring comes early to Temple Square because of the heated facilities under most of the beds. These first offerings were photographed in early March. At this time there is not a lot of color in the gardens, but these brave blossoms promise a profusion of flowers that will lift the hearts of thousands of visitors eager to put dark cold winter behind them. Crocuses have the most courage of all spring flowers. Daffodils, with their faces turned toward the southern sun, follow close behind. The contrast between the drab winter bed and these bright clean colors is startling.

Cunning dwarf iris renew our faith in Christ's message that there is a resurrection and life beyond the grave. Flowers give us hope in the future; they warm our hearts and enrich our lives. All successful gardeners must have hope in large measure. The very nature of their work demands it.

Daffodils and tiny blue chionodoxa dress the bank south of the Temple.

This wonderful spring display was photographed the second week in March. Protected by the Church Office Building on the north, these flowers found the ideal conditions for an early showing.

40

The freshness of yellow, white, and blue colors--the very breath of spring--is a promise of warm crystal-clear days and crisp star-filled nights to come. Rain on these early spring days is welcomed knowing it brings health and vigor to the earth after the freezing dormancy of winter.

Temple Square gardens are just beginning to flower, but by the first week in April the gardens will be resplendent with color. From then on, it will be a nonstop show until mid-October when the gardens are changed for the following spring. The gardeners' work is never ending. They do their work well and reward us handsomely.

41

43

The four large beds surrounding the center fountain on the Grand Plaza in front of the Church Office Building are covered with row cloth during winter months to give the plants a head start for spring. A few days after this picture was taken, the covers were removed exposing a wonderful combination of tulips, pansies, and arabis. Shortly thereafter, different colored aubrietia joins them to enrich the pattern of the gardens. These beds were designed for a continuing floral display through the entire blooming season.

The apricot trees add a graceful lacy effect during early spring and a strong structural statement the rest of the year.

Placed about in the plaza gardens (left) are four life-size bronze statues by Utah sculptors. Dennis Smith produced three of them, and Florence Peterson Hansen created the one of Joseph and Emma. Each depicts some family value taught by the Church.

45

pring days lengthen and the gardens continue to brighten. This is another view of the plaza beds behind the Church Administration Building. The popcorn is popping on the apricot trees. These trees are pruned to give minimum shade so the sun can reach the plants striving to exhibit their beauty. With proper feeding and care, they give their all. Plants are such a wonderful investment; we get so much from the little we give. It is the parable of the mustard seed, a beautiful metaphor for life.

Gardens should be treated like children. Who would think of abusing or punishing a plant with the hope of getting more growth or lovelier blooms?

The Salt Lake Temple seen from the Grand Plaza on the block to the east of it, is a wonderful contrast to the more contemporary architecture of today. This temple is similar to the churches built in eighteenth-century England, and was designed by Truman Angel under the direction of Brigham Young. It was the third temple built by donated labor from early faithful members of the Church. Under construction for forty years, the Temple was completed and dedicated in 1893.

The Temple is a sacred place where only Latter-day Saints in good standing may enter. It is a holy place where families are joined together for time and eternity--husbands to wives and parents to children--and where the same work is done vicariously for those departed souls who cannot do it for themselves. Marriage covenants are made therein, and the gifts of celestial life are explained.

49

50

These naturalized clumps of narcissus are pictured blooming in the beds along each side of the Hawthorn Promenade in front of the Beehive and Lion Houses. Narcissus 'February Gold' and Jack Snipe' boldly watch those passing by.

51

Running west from the Grand Plaza in front of the Church Office Building are two water features called runnels.   These are edged with flower beds and white birch trees. In spring, when the beds are blooming with daffodils, they are reminiscent of the memorable spring scenes in *Doctor Zhivago*.   Left alone, these daffodils have naturalized becoming charming clumps as the bulbs have divided and multiplied.

The stately Beehive House was closed for two years while it was being restored. Today ninety-thousand visitors come each year to see the home where Brigham Young and his family lived. The gardens have been planned to compliment the style and period of the home. Filled with perennial plants, annuals are added to provide constant color during the blooming season.

Roses, lavender, delphinium, digitalis, lavatera, hollyhock, oenothera, campanula, rhubarb, gooseberry, anemone japonica, oriental poppy, iris, buddleia, and hemerocallis are just some of the perennials growing in these gardens. There are also herbs such as chamomile, lemon balm, peppermint, horehound, anise and parsley as well. These gardens are at their loveliest during May and June, but are beautiful during the entire summer.

The Grand Plaza is a fine place to visit. Here you can not only enjoy the beautiful gardens, but the sensitive sculptures and the dramatic Center Fountain.

59

Iceland poppies have recently been planted among the pansies and the purple and pink hyacinths. Tulips have not yet blossomed but will soon join these bright spring offerings. There are windows in the building above this bed that catch the southern winter sun and reflect down heat, warming the soil that sends up early March flowers.

areful study and consideration are given to the rate of colonization along with the sequence and duration of bloom for each plant during the planning and planting stages. This is very important in realizing successful gardens and avoiding what Peter Lassig calls "sputter" (the period of time between planting and blooming).

There are many things to consider beside color and form. For instance, plants at the base of the apricot trees have to be able to thrive in shade with very little moisture as the trees can easily succumb to over watering. However, the outer edges of some plants suffer from intense heat. In the four apricot beds are planted ground covers with needs ranging from dry to moist soil, and sun to shade. Therefore, Lamiastrum, Lamium 'Silver Beacon', Hosta 'Sieboldii', Epimedium 'Sulphurum', Veronica 'Repens', and Sedums 'Dragons Blood', 'Kamtschaticum', and 'Vera Mills' are planted in these beds where their various needs can be met successfully.

61

63

Protected from the city noise, this secluded patio garden is an inviting place to relax and eat lunch. In the evenings it is frequently used for wedding parties. It is filled with abundant color from early spring through fall.

ere are just a few of the spring combinations that come up in April. Arabis 'Snowcap' and Anemone 'Blanda Blue' await tulips' blooms above. Yellow daffodils turn on the light for purple aubrietia surrounding graceful white Narcissus 'Thalia' (upper right).

65

The main north/south axis through Temple Square features six, large, raised flower beds. This is one of the early spring combinations. The colors are like Easter eggs--blue, pink, and yellow while others are red, yellow, and white; or orange, yellow, and blue. For most gardeners, the temptation would be to make all the beds the same. But not here!

The gardens throughout Temple Square are planted in bouquets, each differing from the others. The idea is not to create a sameness but to exemplify the Creator's infinite variety. Thus it surprises us, charms us, and fills us with awe. The combinations are unusual, yet they work well together. They are often playful, but respectful; whimsical, but not frivolous.

The earliest of early tulips, 'Red Emperor', are surrounded by blue pansies. In company with white arabis, they create a patriotic theme. In the background the fountain too, is in full bloom.

70

The values of The Church of Jesus Christ of Latter-day Saints are projected in the bronze statues placed in the Grand Plaza in front of the Church Office Building. All are based on the family unit and the binding of parents and children through eternity. Just as we are the spirit children of a Heavenly Father, so can our children be bound to us forever.

pring flower colors, are always the bright-
est and most clear.

74

ansies, ranunculus, tulips, and narcissus enrich each other through rhythm as well as color.

leeding hearts dance among the narcissus and tulips. These are the plants that were pictured earlier lying on top of the fall garden waiting to be planted. Ample reward!

Spring on Temple Square produces a treasure of color. Pictured left is a delightful clump of Apricot Beauty Tulips.

In the flagpole bed east of the Tabernacle are Tulips 'Red Shine', 'Menton', and 'China Pink' blooming beautifully together.

79

emple Square and the surrounding areas contain over 200 garden beds each with their own unique design. The interesting thing to note is that nowhere do you find flowers planted in rows or straight lines. The flowers look not as if man had planted them, but as if they had chosen to grow where they pleased. These gardens are planned to honor the Creator, not the mortal designer.

In the garden far left, Basket-of-Gold nestles between Broadmoor Junipers. Trailing through the garden are 'Temple of Beauty', 'Queen of Night', and 'Apricot Beauty' Tulips. Pansies 'Joker Light Blue', 'Crystal Bowl Yellow', and 'Luna', as well as Forget-Me-Not 'Early Bird Blue' and purple Lunaria give variety to these flowers that are backed by Viburnum 'Burkwoodii'.

Iceland poppies, pansies, and tulips grow together in exuberant beauty.

Tulips have such class. In the next few pages are pictured some of the seemingly endless varieties that can now be obtained. The Dutch have created an important national industry in the growing and shipping of these glorious spring bulbs. Some are small, while others are as large as one's hand. Some are lily shaped, some fringed, some wrinkled, and some are double resembling the peony. They come in fabulous colors often bordering on the outrageous. There are those that come early, and others that show up later but all are joyfully welcomed. They are most striking when grown in combination with other spring flowers.

The tulips of Temple Square are lifted and stored before summer annuals are planted each year. During the dog days of summer they are cleaned and replanted in certain beds creating a marvelous potpourri the next spring. Nearly 120,000 new bulbs are planted in the rest of the beds

The small courtyard in front of the Lion House has a number of large tubs filled with flowers in monochromatic color schemes. Each tub features one color and each color represents a different value for the young women of the Church. Displayed in every tub is a small sign revealing the value represented.

A little later in spring, these blue Scilla Campanulata bloom and offer a delightful contrast in color to yellow ranunculus. At this time of the year, ranunculus are the most asked-about flower. Their rose-like appearance and delightful colors add magic to the gardens.

The Japanese Tree Peony 'Companion of Serenity', is one of many varieties found on the bank south of the Temple. It is breathtaking when blooming an exquisite pink, as shown here. Others in this bed range from white through deep red.

89

ow-growing pansies and candy tuft nestle under the stately stems of tulips. This combination of colors--pink, orange, rose, purple and white--makes an unusual color pallet.

92

When unpredictable spring weather turns cold, the petals of tulips work as robes which are gathered tightly around their delicate reproductive parts. This process prolongs their beauty. When warmer weather arrives, petals lose this staying power opening and dropping. Tulips are simple and honest. What could be more welcome than a clump of bright spring flowers that magically appears every spring?

93

The varieties of tulips pictured on these pages represer
fraction of the hundreds planted on Temple Square. Because m
of them are grown in soil warmed by garage facilities built bel
the ground, they appear early and attract many flower-hung
visitors from all over the world. These tulips are used with otl
spring flowers in many different ways giving each garden a ch
acter of its own.

95

There is a time when it is no longer spring and not yet summer. It is that time of year when most of us find ourselves at the nursery buying plants and tools. This is a time of major change because the gardens are being replanted with summer annuals. At this time, the gardens are carried by digitalis, iceland poppy, aubrietia, basket-of-gold, arabis, and early perennials such as lupine, delphinium, columbine, iris, peony, and rose. The stewards and volunteers are merciless in their removal of bulbs and the still-valiant pansies. But this must be done if there are to be beautiful beds during the summer months when bulbs are spent and pansies wilt under the hot sun.

Iceland poppy strikes me as one of the most interesting and wondrous of flowers. I marvel at the blooms tightly stuffed into the shells of the buds that when they are opened look like wrinkled clothes just coming out of a suitcase. I love to watch the fragile blooms gently straighten out and flutter in the moving breeze with their transparent colors of cream, yellow, orange, pink, and coral. They remind me of crepe paper or fine silk, and even then I wonder how their long delicate stems can hold up the blooms. The Creator of this universe is full of love to have given us such marvelous gifts.

THE VOLUNTEERS

The demarcation between spring and summer is not as definite as that from winter to spring. Perennials are coming up and some of them are in bloom, but most are just plants growing with a promise. It seems sad to pull out the tulips and pansies that have been so prolific during the past two months, but the job must be done. Mid-May is the time for doing.

Again hundreds of volunteers accomplish in a few hours what the regular gardeners can only achieve in several weeks. Volunteers receive instructions from a garden steward left. The bulbs will be stored according to types--in boxes with their garden location marked on the side so they can be planted again next year. The pansies will be deposited into leaf bags, then dumpsters, and finally taken to the Church greenhouses and dumped for composting.

olunteers sweep up after bags are filled with plants for composting. The volunteer groups come from church membership, and sometimes number in the thousands. Pictured right is a family that has come to work together on a beautiful spring morning. The papa is a member of the gardening staff responsible for coordinating this event. He is communicating on a two-way radio to expedite the work. Each group provides refreshments at the end of the session. All enjoy the camaraderie and feel a sense of accomplishment. They are pleased to have a part in creating the beauty, and afterward they treat the gardens with a sense of ownership.

People from all over the world visit Temple Square and its environs each year, with the majority of them coming in summer. Because these gardens are highly visible, the volunteers take pleasure in helping to make them beautiful.

A gardener supervises to make sure that all perennial plants are left behind. The volunteers learn new plant names, the difference between annuals and perennials, how to prepare the beds, and how to plant. This knowledge, along with the realization that they are needed and useful, is their reward. Volunteers seldom leave without expressing a desire to work longer and return again.

SUM

MER

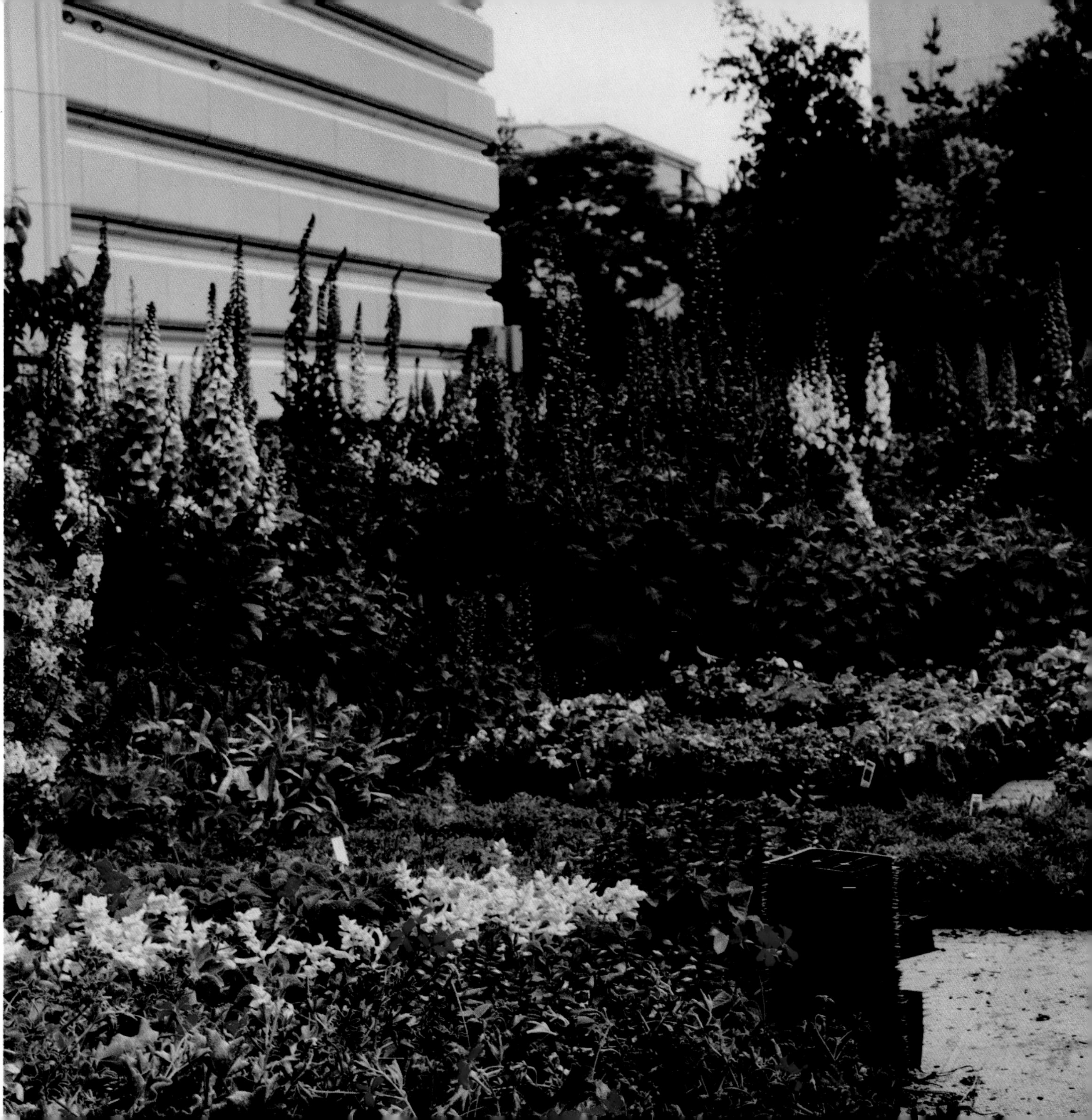

Flats of summer blooming annuals are placed along the sidewalks adjacent to the Lucy Mack Smith garden. This is a crucial time for the newly grown and stripped plants as they must be kept moist from the time of delivery until the designers throw them and they are planted. Gardeners will work in shifts to get the huge job done in time.

There are 180,000 plants grown in the Church greenhouses for summer (an equal number for spring) under the sensitive care of the greenhouse plantsman. Starting quality plants from seed, then nurturing them until they have reached the right stage to leave the greenhouse for hardening off and delivered to be transplanted requires great skill and devoted attention. The plants sent to Temple Square have received an abundance of both.

Spires of digitalis and delphinium, along with Achillia 'The Pearl' keep the show running during this replacement period.

105

ome of the flowers that create the magic in the Lucy Mack Smith Garden while summer annuals are beginning to take hold are hundreds of foxglove, stands of iceland poppies, and iris.

The days are moving toward the summer solstice and we can enjoy these flowers that return each year without replanting. Lupine, delphinium, and foxglove unite in tall spires of color. When they have finished blooming at the end of June, they are cut to the ground. As soon as the weather begins to cool off in August, the delphinium and digitalis send up wonderful color spikes again though less dramatic and fewer in number.

Early day lilies begin blooming in June. Their graceful foliage gives structure all season, but the month of July is when they fill the gardens with their form and color.

109

III

These are just a few varieties of iris that bloom in several of the gardens during May and June.

Some of the blooms of early summer: the rose, the daisy, and the day lily are near perfection.

114

W hat an unusual bloom Allium 'Gigantium' is! A sphere composed of hundreds of tiny individual blossoms that know just how long to grow in order to make a perfect ball.

It's impossible not to be impressed by the elegant use of color in the honeysuckle 'Goldflame'.

eace is the name of this rose. Roses flourish in this high and arid desert. There is a prophesy that the people who came to this area would make the desert blossom as the rose. Brigham Young colonized communities from Canada to the Pacific coast. He visualized a self-sufficient peace-loving people living in what was then called Deseret. The name, Deseret, means honey bee, and is a symbol found on many early architectural features. When Deseret was given statehood it was renamed Utah after the Ute Indians from this area.

osmos are such happy flowers! Their open form and cheerful colors say "summer" in a most delightful way. The variety growing at the base of this statue is 'Sonata Dwarf Mix'.

Summer temperatures in this high desert can go well above the century mark. Keeping the gardens green and growing, especially in this hotter than average downtown location, can be difficult. Once again, the gardeners, the volunteers, and the maintenance people are dedicated to their work.

One of the most colorful parts of the garden is this small section just behind the administration building which houses the president of the Church of Jesus Christ of Later Day Saints and the twelve apostles. In the photograph to the left, we are looking toward the new administration building through an impressive bloom of cleome. These give the impression of an exploding forth of July fireworks display. Once they start to bloom, they will keep going nearly all summer.

The other plantings that support the base of the cleome are petunias, geraniums, snap dragons, marigolds, and ageratum. The color is dazzling!

The Seagull Monument on Temple Square commemorates an event that occurred the first year the pioneers entered the Great Salt Lake Valley. They arrived on July 24, 1847 and immediately began planting crops. When the young plants looked promising, great hoards of crickets began devouring them. The settlers battled valiantly to save their only means of survival, but to no avail. When they were in the deepest despair over their hopeless situation--after praying that a miracle would save their precious crops--seagulls from the shores of the Great Salt Lake swooped down in such numbers they obscured the sun. Consuming the crickets, they rushed to the lake to empty their bellies, then repeated the process over and over until the crickets were destroyed. This literally saved the lives of those early church members. The story is inscribed on the sides of this monument explaining why the seagull is the Utah state bird.

This ornamental cabbage is masquerading as a flower.

The Bride's Tree as this honeysuckle tree is known is the favorite spot for recording wedding days.

125

One of the sacred ordinances performed in the Temple is the uniting of marriage partners for time and eternity. The gardens around the Temple provide a beautiful background for photographing these couples on their important day. The ceremony, a simple exchange of vows and covenants, is attended only by family members and a few close friends.

The picture to the left is of the perennial border between the Tabernacle and the Assembly Hall. Prolific Dianthus 'Tiny Rubies' forms a ground cover with Love-in-a-Mist 'Persian Jewels' growing up through it.

Above, heliotrope, marigolds and vinca combine delightfully.

Begonia, fern, and coleus are all plants that love shade and form this garden on the north side of the South Visitors' Center. Lush and vibrant with color, this garden is as pleasant from within the glass wall as from without. It is an exhilarating, and fitting base for the majestic glass curtain that reflects the Temple and other gardens of the square.

128

129

Pinwheel zinnias, yellow marigolds, and ageratum harmonize together above, while Echo blue lisianthus and Veronica geraniums sing a different song.

132

It is appropriate that the bronze statue of
Joseph and Emma Smith should be situated next
to the President's Garden.

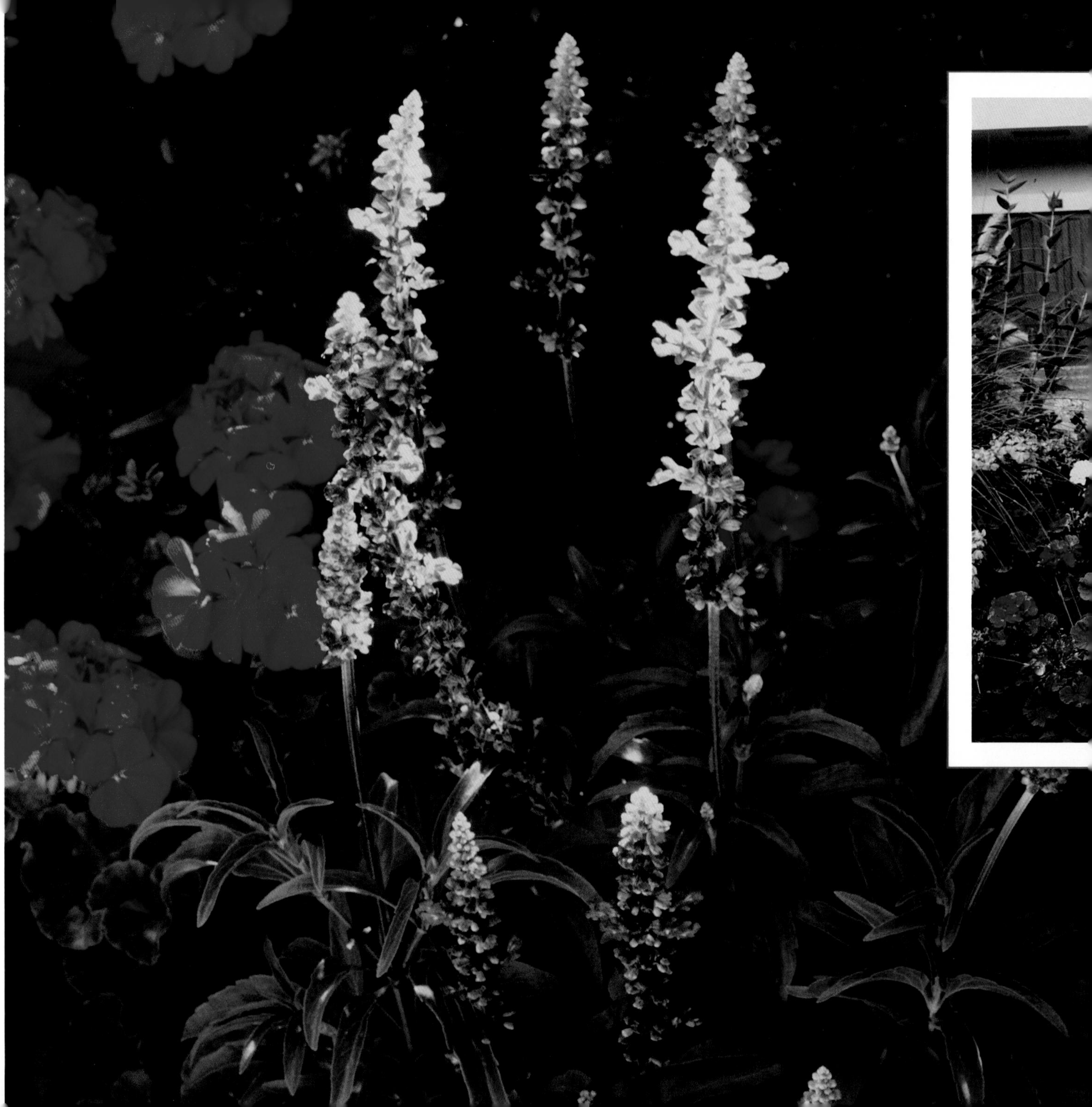

ith the Tabernacle in the background, Green fountain grass and blue salvia provide structural rama.

ehind the Boxwood hedge, right, is the Rose Garden. The beds inside are filled with annuals that apture the eye when temperatures become too hot for roses to bloom.

I realize there are flower lovers who prefer gardens planted in neat rows of the same variety and color. My favorite car wash has a mound in front with the words, "COME CLEAN," in dusty miller. I do not criticize this approach. I draw a comparison to New York's Rockettes who do those wonderful synchronized tap dances. But flowers forced to create a large design are, in my view, less natural and lovely. It is the Disneyland approach with Mickey showing the time and date.

The English garden is more appealing to me. With this style, each flower can be appreciated more easily for its unique beauty. As you can see from the picture above, the flowers are planted in a collective expression of scale and color. A combination of flowers, like a chorus, can blend voices to render more than one note. Then the garden becomes a choir of harmony

The flowers that combine to create the floral bouquet, above, are Lisianthus 'Heidi Yellow', Geranium 'Appleblossom', Heliotrope 'Marine', Salvia 'Victoria Blue', and Sanvitalia 'Mandarin Orange'.

Red Fountain grass creates the fountain effect in this bed between catalpa trees.

Early morning sun lights up these Zinnia 'Linara'. The use of yellow-orange flowers will lighten any arrangement.

id you ever wonder what to plant in a shade garden? This one behind the Beehive and Lion Houses is spectacular in late summer. Impatiens, fern, begonias, ivy, geraniums, and browallia grow prolifically. This tea garden surrounds the patio where guests from the Lion House Pantry lunch. In the evening, wedding parties often gather in celebration. The Lion House was constructed in 1859 by Brigham Young, who was a carpenter by trade. His houses were built with the best materials available and were of the finest craftsmanship.

The Church Office Building (behind the wall) is where many hundreds of workers have their offices. The secluded garden here is a welcomed relief from the asphalt and cement that is downtown Salt Lake City. It is a wonderful reminder of a bygone day when the Young residence was one of the largest structures in the area. Now a museum, the house is visited by ninety-thousand visitors each year.

141

The first week in October finds the garden beds at their best. Here blue salvia, geraniums, begonias, petunias, coleus, and marigolds are bursting with color. Because these beds immediately surround the Temple, they are only viewed by newly-married couples and their guests. The combinations of flowers and careful tending makes these floral displays a visual feast.

JUST GREEN

145

eedless to say, blooms do not cover all of the grounds on Temple Square. Lawns and ground covers carpet spaces under trees, between beds, and among flowers.

We show a few examples used throughout the gardens. Clockwise, from upper left, are pictured Lamium 'Silver Beacon,' Campanula 'Poscharskyana', Tradescantia, Fern 'Ostrich Plume', Dianthus 'Raspberry Parfait', and Hosta 'Blue Peter'.

146

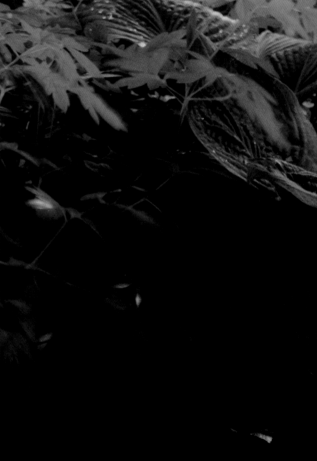

148

nd finally, we present the unusual coleus, the wild card of the gardens at Temple Square. Where shade is a problem and color is needed, coleus is the answer. And just look at the colors! Rust, red, pink, chartreuse, green, gold, yellow, and white are found in wondrous combination.

This book began as a gift for my wife to commemorate her work as a gardener at Temple Square. At first it was kept secret from her, but as the project developed, the size and contents of the gardens became so overwhelming that I needed to ask her for information. There are thousands of plants and hundreds of varieties growing in these gardens that cover more than two blocks in downtown Salt Lake City. This book contains only a fraction of what is grown at Temple Square. It would be impossible to show every plant and flower of beauty and interest. But I hope this collection represents the feeling you find here, and the philosophy behind the gardens. In the last section of the book, I have included a list of the plants and their varieties for each picture shown.

Most of the photographs were taken by me. There are a couple taken by my son, Zeke, and a few by my good friend, Jim Kent. The bridal couple was photographed by Drake Busath and is used here with permission. I do not consider myself a professional, but I take great pleasure in some of these photographs. Some of the shots were beginners luck; others can be attributed to good film, good processing (by Borge B. Andersen), and great subjects. For those who are curious about the photography, I used a Mamiya M645 pro camera with a two and a quarter format using 120 Varicolor negative, or Kodak Elite color transparency film. For the most part I used a 50 mm macro lens for the close up photos and a 35mm wide angle lens for the larger space shots showing buildings and trees. Most of the pictures were taken with the smallest possible aperture, with longer exposures to get the most detail. (This became a bit of a problem because the downtown location is usually a little breezy. Often, I had to wait several minutes for the breezes to quiet down and the blossoms to stop moving.)

One of the most impressive things about these gardens is that such a small staff creates and cares for all this visual beauty. I thank them and the Church of Jesus Christ of Latter-day Saints for beautifying my city. Thanks too, must be given to the garden guides who provide the free tours from April 1st through October 7th. They give so freely of their time both as volunteer gardeners and as tour guides. Their love of this wonderful creation is a testimony to their faith.

Temple Square is one of the busiest tourist attractions in the United States. Six million people visit here each year. All of the attractions, tours, films, broadcasts, and concerts on the Square are given without charge. One can even obtain a Book of Mormon free upon request.

I hope you have enjoyed looking through these pages as much as I have enjoyed producing them. It has been inspiring to closely observe the color, the variety, and the vitality that make the gardens what they are.

151

# NOTES

152

THE COMBINATIONS

1

Following are the names of the plants pictured on each page.

2	2	3	7	10
	PAPAVER ORINTALE 'SALMON' (ORIENTAL POPPY)	CLEOME 'QUEEN MIX'	CHRYSANTHEMUM 'BRISTOL DAISY WHITE'	CABBAGE 'COLOR-UP WI
		SALVIA 'VICTORIA BLUE'	CHRYSANTHEMUM 'BRISTOL DAISY ROSE'	CABBAGE 'COLOR-UP R
		MARIGOLD 'FIRST LADY'		SALVIA 'VICTORIA BLU
		PETUNIA 'LILAC SUPER CASCADE'		ZINNIA 'PINWHEEL RC
		BEGONIA 'WINGS MIXED'		CHRYSANTHEMUM 'BRIS ROSE'
		PETUNIA 'TOTAL MADNESS MIX'		

11	12	13	14
OSE 'QUEEN ELIZABETH'	IMPATIENS 'ELFIN MIX'	ROSE 'CHI CAGO PEACE' ANEMONE JAPONICA 'HONORINE JOBERT'	IMPATIENS 'ELFIN MIX'

3

15	18	21	36
PHYSOSTEGIA VIRGINIANA 'VIRGINIA ROSE' (FALSE DRAGONS HEAD, OBEDIENT PLANT) BRUNNERA MACROPHYLLA (PERENNIAL FORGET-ME-NOT) COSMOS 'SONATA MIX' ARTEMESIA 'POWIS CASTLE' (DUSTY MILLER) CHRYSANTHEMUM 'BRISTOL DAISY ROSE' CHRYSANTHEMUM 'BRISTOL DAISY WHITE'	ALTHAEA 'TALL SINGLE PINK' (HOLLYHOCK) IPOMEA 'HEAVENLY BLUE' (IPOMOEA)	ARTEMISIA 'POWIS CASTLE' (DUSTY MILLER) CHRYSANTHEMUM 'BRISTOL DAISY ROSE' CHRYSANTHEMUM 'SUNDORO' PHYSOSTEGIA VIRGINIANA 'VIRGINIA ROSE' (FALSE DRAGONSHEAD, OBEDIENT PLANT) 'STACHYS BYZANTINA' (LAMBS EAR) COREOPSIS 'ZAGREB' (TICKSEED) BRUNERA MACROPHYLLA 'PERENNIAL FORGET-ME -NOT"	GIANT CROCUS 'MIX COLORS'

4

38	39	40	42
DWARF IRIS 'RETICULATA HARMONY'	ARABIS 'SNOWCAP'	GIANT CROCUS 'MIXED COLORS'	GIANT CROCUS 'YELLOW MAMMOTH'
	NARCISSUS 'GERANIUM'		
	NARCISSUS ' STAINLESS'		
	NARCISSUS 'THALIA'		
	NARCISSUS 'TREVITHIAN'		
	NARCISSUS 'W.P. MILNER'		
	PANSY 'MAXIM MARINE'		
	PANSY 'MAXIM SHERBET'		
	VIOLA 'KING HENRY'		
	NARCISSUS 'JULES VERNE'		
	CHIONODOXA 'BLUE'		

5

43

NARCISSUS 'JULES VERNE'

CHIONODOXA 'BLUE'

44

TULIP 'TORONTO'

ARABIS 'SNOWCAP'

PANSY 'UNIVERSAL YELLOW'

PANSY 'IMPERIAL BLUE'

PANSY 'JUNG FRAU'

PANSY 'CROWN AZURE BLUE'

PANSY 'CLEAR SKY PURPLE'

46

ARABIS 'SNOWCAP'

TULIP 'TORONTO'

PANSY 'UNIVERSAL YELLOW BLOTCH'

PANSY 'IMPERIAL BLUE'

PANSY 'MAJESTIC GIANT PURPLE'

PANSY 'BLACK DEVIL'

47

ROSE 'EDEN'

6

48	49	50	51
ARABIS SNOWCAP'	ARABIS 'SNOWCAP'	SCILLA 'SIBERICA'	NARCISSUS 'JACK SNIPE'
TULIP 'TORONTO'	PANSY 'TRUE BLUE'	NARCISSUS 'FEBRUARY GOLD'	SCILLA 'SIBERICA'
PANSY 'UNIVERSAL YELLOW BLOTCH'		NARCISSUS 'JACK SNIPE'	
PANSY 'TURE BLUE'			
PANSY 'UNIVERSAL BLUE BLOTCH'			
PANSY 'IMPERIAL BLUE'			

7

52	54	55	56
NARCISSUS 'UNSURPASSABLE'	HYDRANGEA 'MERRITT PINK'	NARCISSUS 'FEBRUARY GOLD'	TULIP 'PINUP'
			TULIP 'SPRING GREE
ARABIS 'SNOWCAP'		NARCISSUS 'JACK SNIPE'	TULIP 'ELIZABETH AR
			PANSY 'JUNG FRAU
TULIP 'TORONTO'		SCILLA 'SIBERICA'	PANSY 'MAXIM SHER
			PANSY 'YELLOW SPLA
PANSY 'IMPERIAL BLUE'			PANSY 'IMPERIAL BL
PANSY 'CLEAR SKY PURPLE'			
			TULIP 'ASTA NIELSE
			TULIP 'BLUE BELL
			TULIP 'SMILING QUE
			TULIP 'VARINAS'
			PANSY 'CROWN AZU
			PANSY 'CRYSTAL BO
			DEEP BLUE'
			PANSY 'JUNG FRA
			PANSY 'LUNA'
			PANSY 'UNIVERSA
			YELLOW'

8

57	58	59	60	
ARABIS 'SNOWCAP'	HYACINTH 'CARNEIGE'	PAPAVER NUDICAULE 'WONDERLAND YELLOW' ('ICELAND POPPPY)	ARABIS 'SNOWCAP'	*9*
TULIP 'MRS. MOON'	HYACINTH 'AMETHYST'	HYACINTH 'PINK PEARL'	TULIP 'APRICOT BEAUTY'	
TULIP 'APRICOT BEAUTY'	PANSY ' UNIVERSAL BLUE BLOTCH'	HYACINTH 'AMETHYST'	TULIP 'ELIZABETH ARDEN'	
TULIP 'MRS. SHEEPERS'	VIOLA 'JERSY GEM'	PANSY 'MAJESTIC GIANT PURPLE'	TULIP 'TORONTO'	
PANSY 'IMPERIAL BLUE'		PANSY 'IMPERIAL PINK SHADES'	'PANSY 'IMPERIAL BLUE'	
PANSY 'UNIVERSAL TRUE BLUE' PANSY 'ROCCOCO MIX'		PANSY 'MELODY PURPLE'	PANSY 'UNIVERSAL YELLOW BLOTCH'	
			PANSY 'UNIVERSAL BLUE BLOTCH'	
			PANSY 'CLEAR SKY PURPLE'	
			PANSY 'UNIVERSAL TRUE BLUE'	
RANUNCULUS 'BLOOMINGDALE PINK'			PANSY 'BLACK DEVIL'	
			PANSY 'LUNA'	

61	62	63	64
PAPAVER NUDICAULE 'WONDERLAND YELLOW' (ICELAND POPPY) PANSY 'CRYSTAL BOWL DEEP YELLOW'	KALANCHOE 'PINK' FERN 'SPRENGERI' PANSY 'CRYSTAL BOWL ROSE'	DICENTRA SPECTABILIS 'PINK' (BLEEDING HEART) AUBRIETIA 'MONARCH STRAIN' TULIP 'BLUSHING MAID' TULIP 'GEORGETTE' TULIP 'BILLBOARD' TULIP 'GUDOSHNIK' TULIP 'OSCAR' TULIP 'PANDOUR' TULIP 'TEMPLE OF BEAUTY' NARCISSUS 'FORTISSIMO' NARCISSUS 'GERANIUM' NARCISSUS 'PIPIT' NARCISSUS 'SWEET SERENADE'	ANEMONE 'BLAND BLUE' ARABIS 'SNOWCAP'

10

65	66	68	69
AUBRIETIA 'MONARCH STRAIN'	HYACINTH 'PEARLE BRILLIANTE'	FORSYTHIA 'GOLD ZAUBER'	ARABIS 'SNOWCAP'
ARABIS 'SNOWCAP'	HYACINTH 'DELFT BLUE'		TULIP 'TORONTO'
NARCISSUS 'THALIA	HYACINTH 'BLUE MAGIC'	ARABIS 'SNOWCAP'	TULIP 'ROSY WINGS'
RCISSUS 'UNSURPASSABLE'	HYACINTH 'PINK DIAMOND'		TULIP 'APRICOT BEAUTY'
	HYACINTH 'PINK PEARL'	TULIP 'RED EMPEROR'	TULIP 'MRS MOON'
	PANSY 'JUNG FRAU'		TULIP 'ELIZABETH ARDEN'
	PANSY 'UNIVERSAL DEEP YELLOW'	PANSY 'CRYSTAL BOWL YELLOW'	TULIP 'GUDOSHNIK'
AUBRIETIA 'MONARCH STRAIN'			TULIP 'SPRING GREEN'
RCISSUS 'UNSURPASSABLE'	PANSY 'AZURE BLUE'	PANSY 'JUNG FRAU'	PANSY 'IMPERIAL BLUE'
	PANSY 'CRYSTAL BLOW DEEP BLUE		PANSY 'UNIVERSAL YELLOW BLOTCH'
		PANSY 'LUNA'	PANSY 'CLEAR SKY PURPLE'
ARABIS 'SNOW CAP'	PANSY 'UNIVERSAL LIGHT BLUE'		
AUBRIETIA 'MONARCH STRAIN'	PANSY 'CRYSTAL BOWL ROSE'		
	PANSY 'LUNA'		

11

12

70

TULIP 'MRS. MOON'

TULIP 'GUDOSHNIK'

TULIP 'APRICOT BEAUTY'

ARABIS 'SNOWCAP'

PANSY 'ROCCOCO MIX'

PANSY 'UNIVERSAL TRUE BLUE'

PANSY 'BLACK DEVIL'

PANSY 'UNIVERSAL YELLOW BLOTCH'

PANSY 'IMPERIAL BLUE'

PANSY 'CROWN AZURE BLUE'

71

TULIP 'MRS. MOON'

TULIP 'APRICOT BEAUTY'

TULIP 'ELIZABETH ARDEN'

TULIP 'GUDOSHNIK'

ARABIS 'SNOWCAP'

AURINIA SAXATILE 'GOLD DUST" (BASKET OF GOLD)'

PANSY 'MAJESTIC GIANT PURPLE'

PANSY 'CROWN AZURE'

PANSY 'UNIVERSAL BLUE BLOTCH'

PANSY 'UNIVERSAL YELLOW BLOTCH'

72

NARCISSUS 'GERANIUM'

PANSY 'JOKER LIGHT BLUE'

AURINIA SAXATILE 'GOLD DUST' (BASKET OF GOLD)

73

AURINIA SAXATILE 'GOLD DUST' (BASKET OF GOLD)

TULIP 'GOLDEN APELDOORN'

NARCISSUS 'GERANIU

PANSY 'JOKER LIGH BLUE'

74	76	77	78
PANSY 'ROCCOCO MIX'	DICENTRA SPECTABILIS 'PINK' (BLEEDING HEART)	TULIP 'TEMPLE OF BEAUTY'	AURINIA SAXATILE 'GOLD DUST' (BASKET OF GOLD)'
ANSY 'UNIVERSAL VIOLET'	NARCISSUS 'FORTISSIMO'	TULIP 'HOCUS POCUS'	AUBRIETIA 'MONARCH STRAIN'
	NARCISSUS 'SWEET HARMONY'	TULIP 'QUEEN OF NIGHT'	ARABIS 'SNOWCAP'
ARCISSUS 'MOUNT HOOD'	NARCISSUS 'GERANIUM'		NARCISSUS 'THALIA'
	TULIP 'DORRIE OVERALL'	TULIP 'BILLBOARD'	PANSY 'CRYSTAL BOWL YELLOW'
		PANSY 'CLEAR SKY PURPLE'	
		PANSY 'CROWN AZURE'	PANSY 'JUNG FRAU'
RANUNCULUS 'BLOOMINGDALE RED'		PANSY 'JOKER LIGHT BLUE'	
RANUNCULUS BLOOMINGDALE YELLOW'		PANSY 'LUNA'	
PANSY 'JUNG FRAU'		PANSY 'JUNG FRAU'	
PANSY ' CRYSTAL BOWL		PANSY 'UNIVERSAL LIGHT BLUE'	
PRIMROSE 'YELLOW '		PANSY 'UNIVERSAL TRUE BLUE'	

13

79	80	81	82
RANUNCULAUS 'BLOOMINGDALE MIX'	VIBURNUM 'BURKWOODII	PAPAVER NUDICAULE "WONDRLAND MIXED' (ICELAND POPPY)	TULIP 'DREAMLAND
TULIP 'APRICOT BEAUTY'	TULIP 'TEMPLE OF BEAUTY'		TULIP 'LILAC PERFECTI
TULIP 'SMILING QUEEN	TULIP 'APRICOT BEAUTY'	PANSY 'IMPERIAL PINK'	TULIP 'MRS. MOON'
RANUNCULUS 'BLOOMINGDALE MIX'	TULIP 'QUEEN OF NIGHT'		TULIP 'WHITE DREAM
VIOLA 'JERSEY GEM'	LUNARIA 'BIENNIS PURPLE		DICENTRA SPECTABIL 'PINK' (BLEEDING HEA
PANSY 'UNIVERSAL TRUE BLUE'	AURINIA SAXATILE 'GOLD DUST'		PANSY 'IMPERIAL BLU
PANSY 'UNIVERSAL YELLOW BLOTCH'	AURINIA SAXATILE CITRINUM 'SILVER QUEEN'		PANSY 'CRYSTAL BOW DEEP BLUE'
PANSY 'CROWN AZURE BLUE'	MYOSOTIS 'EARLY BIRD BLUE (FORGET- ME- NOT)'		PANSY 'IMPERIAL ANTIQUE SHADES'
PANSY 'UNIVERSAL YELLOW'	PANSY 'JOKER LIGHT BLUE'		PANSY 'CLEAR SKY PURPLE'
PANSY 'CRYSTAL BOWL DEEP BLUE'	PANSY ' CRYSTAL BOWL YELLOW'		PANSY 'MAJESTIC GIA PURPLE'
TULIP 'CHINA PINK' TULIP 'RED SHINE' TULIP 'MENTON'			PANSY 'UNIVERSAL DE YELLOW'

14

84	85	86	87
TULIP 'APRICOT BEAUTY'	HYDRANGEA 'MERRITT PINK'	SCILLA CAMPANULATA 'BLUE' (ENGLISH WOOD HYACINTH)	JAPANESE TREE PEONY 'COMPANION OF SERENITY'
TULIP 'ROSY WINGS'	AUBRIETIA 'MONARCH STRAIN'	RANUNCULUS 'BLOOMINGDALE YELLOW'	
PAPAVER NUDICAULE 'CHAMPAIGN BUBBLES' (ICELAND POPPY)	PANSY 'CLEAR SKY PURPLE'		
RANUNCULUS BLOOMINGDALE MIXED'	ARABIS 'SPRING CHARM'		
MYOSOTIS "EARLY BIRDBLUE' (FORGET-ME-NOT)	LILIUM 'EASTER LILY'		
PANSY 'CRYSTAL BOWL YELLOW'	HYDRANGEA 'MERRITT WHITE'		
PANSY 'BABY LUCIA'	ARABIS 'SNOWCAP'		
PANSY ' IMPERIAL BLUE'	PANSY 'LUNA'		
PANSY 'MELODY ROSE WITH BLOTCH'			
VIOLA 'JONNY JUMP-UP'			

15

88	90	91	92
ARABIS 'SNOWCAP'	AURINIA SAXITILE 'GOLD DUST' (BASKET OF GOLD)	ARABIS 'SNOWCAP'	FORSYTHIA 'GOLD ZAU
TULIP 'ANGELIQUE'	LUNARIA BIENNIS 'PURPLE'	TULIP LINNARA BATTALINI 'RED GEM'	TULIP 'RED EMPERO
TULIP 'CHINA PINK'	LUNARIA BIENNIS 'WHITE"	PANSY 'IMPERIAL PINK SHADES'	PANSY 'CRYSTAL B OV YELLOW'
TULIP 'RENOWN'		VIOLA 'KING HENRY'	PANSY 'JUNG FRAU
TULIP 'MRS. J.T. SCHEEPERS'			PANSY 'LUNA'
TULIP 'MENTON'			PANSY 'IMPERIAL ORA
PANSY 'UNIVERSAL DEEP YELLOW'		TULIP 'OXFORD ELITE	PANSY 'MAJESTIC GIA PURPLE'
PANSY 'LUNA'		MYOSOTIS 'EARLY BIRD BLUE' (FORGET-ME-NOT)	VIOLA 'KING HENR
PANSY 'IMPERIAL ORANGE'		LUNARIA BIENNIS 'PURPLE'	TULIP 'ASTA NIELSE
PANSY 'CRYSTAL BOWL DEEP BLUE'		PANSY 'MAJESTIC GIANT PURPLE '	TULIP 'PINK IMPRESSI
		PANSY 'IMPERIAL FROSTY PINK'	PANSY 'CRYSTAL BOV PRIMROSE YELLOW
		IRIS SIBERICA 'CEASAR'S BROTHER'	PANSY 'IMPERIAL BLU
			PANSY 'CRYSTAL BOWL BLUE'

16

93	94	95	96
TULIP 'PINK IMPRESSION'	TULIP 'BUGUNDY LACE'	TULIP 'SWEET HARMONY'	PAPAVER NUDICAULE 'CHAMPAIGN BUBBLES' (ICELAND POPPY)
TULIP 'ASTA NIELSON'	TULIP 'MRS. MOON'	TULIP 'QUEEN OF NIGHT'	
	LUNARIA BIENNIS 'PURPLE'	TULIP 'DREAMLAND'	
		TULIP 'BURGUNDY LACE'	
		LUNARIA BIENNIS 'PURPLE'	
	TULIP 'HOCUS POCUS'	LUNARIA BIENNIS 'WHITE'	
		PANSY 'IMPERIAL PINK' SHADES'	
	TULIP 'OSCAR'		
	PANSY 'CRYSTAL BOWL PURPLE'	TULIP 'TEXAS FLAME' RANUNCULUS 'BLOOMIN GDALE YELLOW AND RED'	
		PANSY ' JUNG FRAU'	
		PANSY 'CRYSTAL BOWL PRIMROSE YELLOW'	

17

102

HEUCHERA 'BRESSINGHAM HYBRIDS' (CORAL BELLS)

103

IRIS 'EVENING ECHO'

104

FOXFLOVE 'GIANT SHIRLEY' (DIGITALIS)

DELPHINIUM 'SUMMER SKIES'

ACHILLEA 'THE PEARL' (YARROW)

IN FLATS:

SALVIA 'LADY IN RED'

SALVIA 'EMPIRE SERIES'

PETUNIA 'MIXED'

106

FOXGLOVE 'GIANT SHIRLEY' (DIGITALIS)

18

107	108	109	110	
PAPAVER NUDICAULE 'WONDERLAND PINK' (ICELAND POPPY)	DIGITALIS 'GIANT SHIRLEY' (FOXGLOVE)	HEMEROCALLIS' 'GERTRUDE CONDON' (DAY LILY)	IRIS 'ORANGE PARADE'	
PAPAVER NUDICAULE 'WONDERLAND YELLOW' (ICELAND P OPPY)	LUPINUS 'RUSSEL STAIN' (LUPINE)			*19*
DELPHINIUM 'GIANT PACIFIC'				
IRIS 'SUNDAY CHIMES"				

111	112	113	114
IRIS 'CEASAR'S BROTHER' IRIS 'BAVARIAN CREAM' IRIS 'YELLOW CURLS' IRIS 'EASTER TIME'	HEMEROCALLIS 'RED LANDSCAPE SUPREME' (DAY LILY)	ROSE 'CHERISH' CHRYSANTHEMUM 'SNOW LADY' (DAISY) ROSE 'MCGREADY'S SUNSET" ROSE 'CHINA DOLL'	LONICERA HECKROT 'GOLD FLAME HONE SUCKLE'

20

115	116	118	120
ALLIUM 'GIGANTEUM'	ROSE 'PEACE'	COSMOS 'DWARF SONATA MIXED'	CLEOME 'QUEEN PINK'
		GERANIUM 'ORBIT APPLEBLOSSOM'	
		CHRYSANTHEMUM 'PALUDOSUM SNOWLAND'	
		CHRYSANTHEMUM 'DAHLBERG DAISY'	

21

	123	124	126	127
22	CABBAGE 'COLOR-UP PINK' CHRYSANTHEMUM 'BRISTOL DAISY ROSE"	LONICERA KOROLKOWII (BLUELEAF HONEYSUCKLE)	NIGELLA 'PERSIAN JEWELS' (LOVE-IN-THE-MIST) DIANTHUS 'TINY RUBIES'	HELIOTROPE 'MARIN MARIGOLD 'JANIE YELLOW' VINCA 'PRETTY IN RO ZINNIA 'PETER PAN M

128	130	131	132
STAR MAGNOLIA (SHRUB)	MARIGOLD 'INCA GOLD'	LISIANTHUS 'ECHO BLUE'	CLEOME 'QUEEN MIX'
BERGINIA CORDIFOLIA 'PERFECTA'	MARIGOLD 'EARLY SPICE SAFFRON'	LISIANTHUS 'ECHO PINK'	MARIGOLD 'FIRST LADY'
EGONIA 'FRILLY PINK'	MARIGOLD 'LEMON GEM'	GERANIUM 'ORBIT ROSE'	ARTEMESIA 'MARITIMA DIAMOND' (DUSTY MILLER)
BEGONIA 'LINDA'	AGERATUM 'BLUE HORIZON'	CANTERBURY BELLS 'BLUE'	SALVIA 'VICTORIA BLUE'
BEGONIA 'VIVA'	ZINNIA 'PINWHEEL ROSE'		PETUNIA 'MADNESS MIX'
COLEUS 'WIZARD MIX'	SALVIA 'VICTORIA BLUE'		GERANIUM 'ORBIT MIX'
BEROUS BEGONIA 'NON-STOP MIX'			COLEUS 'WIZARD MIX'
BEROUS BEGONIA 'NON STOP ROSE PINK'			
BEROUS BEGONIA 'PIN-UP MIX"			
FERN 'BOSTON'			

23

	133	134	135	136
24	SCILLA CAMPANULA TA (ENGLISH WOOD HYACINTH) RANUNCULUS 'BLOOMINGDALE SCARLET'	SALVIA 'VICTORIA BLUE' GERANIUM 'VERONICA'	'FOUNTAIN GRASS 'GREEN' SALVIA 'VICTORIA BLUE' GERANIUM 'VERONICA' GERANIUM 'BRIGHT EYES' MARIGOLD 'INCA GOLD' MARIGOLD 'GOLDEN GEM' GERANIUM 'ORBIT MIX' GERANIUM 'SHOWGIRL' GERANIUM 'ORBIT MIX' PETUNIA 'SUPER CASCADE WHITE' PETUNIA 'SUPER CASCADE RED' PETUNIA 'HAPPINESS' PETUNIA 'CHIFFON CASCADE' PETUNIA 'ULTRA SALMON' PETUNIA 'APPLEBLOSSOM'	FOUNTAIN GRASS 'G ARTEMESIA 'SILVER I (DUSTY MILLER) GERANIUM 'CAMI GERANIUM 'ORBI SCARLET' MARIGOLD 'FIRST L NIEREMBERGIA 'PU ROBE' PETUNIA 'SUPERMA CORAL' VERBENA 'PEACHES CREAM' HYPOESTES 'CONFE ROSE' SCAEVOLA 'BLUE W DER' VINCA 'CARPET M

137	138	139	140	
ROSE 'BALLERINA'	LISIANTHUS 'HEIDI YELLOW'	FOUNTAIN GRASS 'RED'	FERN 'BOSTON'	
	GERANIUM 'ORBIT APPLEBLOSSOM'	COREOPSIS 'SUNRAY	IMPATIENS 'ELFIN MIX'	
	GERANIUM 'VERONICA'	ARTEMESIA 'MARITIMA' (DUSTY MILLER)	IMPATIENS 'BLITZ MIX'	
LVIA 'VICTORIA WHITE'	SNAPDRAGON 'ROCKET PINK'	GERANIUM 'ORBIT MIX'	COLEUS 'WIZARD MIX'	25
LVIA 'EMPIRE PURPLE'	SALVIA 'VICTORIA BLUE'	PETUNIA 'MADNESS MIX'		
LVIA 'EMPIRE WHITE'	HELIOTROPE 'MARINE'			
ANIUM 'ORBIT HOT PINK'	SANVITALIA 'MANDARIN ORANGE'			
ERANIUM 'ORBIT PINK'		ZINNIA 'LINARA'		
GERANIUM 'ORBIT APPLEBLOSSOM'				

	142	146	147	148
26	GERANIUM 'VERONICA' ZINNIA 'LINARA' SALVIA 'VICTORIA BLUE' BEGONIA 'KINGS MIX' IMPATIENS 'ELFIN RED' TUBEROUS BEGONIA 'PIN-UP MIX' ROSE 'CHICAGO PEACE'	LAMIUM 'SILVER BEACON'	CAMPANULA 'POSCHARSKYANA' TRADISCANTIA (SPIDERWORT) DIANTHUS 'RASPBERRY PARFAIT' HOSTA 'BLUE PETER'	COLEUS 'WIZARD M BEGONIA 'VIVA' BEGONIA 'LINDA BEGONIA 'SCARLET COLEUS 'PARK'S BRILLIANT MIX' BEGONIA TUBERO 'NON-STOP ORANG NIEREMBERGIA 'PU ROBE' BEGONIA 'WINGS R COLEUS 'WIZARI SUNSET' GERANIUM 'ORBIT I HELIOTROPE 'MA R

149 | 150

COLEUS 'WIZARD MIX'

BEGONIA 'VIVA'

ALVIA 'VICTORIA BLUE'

COLEUS 'WIZARD JADE'

GERATUM 'BLUE BLAZER'

SALVIA ARGENTA

27